≠

pray me stay eager

≠ *pray me stay eager* ≠

ELLEN DORÉ WATSON

ALICE JAMES BOOKS *Farmington, Maine*

10 9 8 7 6 5 4 3 2 1

Alice James Books are published by Alice James Poetry Cooperative,
Inc., an affiliate of the University of Maine at Farmington.

Alice James Books
114 Prescott Street
Farmington, ME 04938
www.alicejamesbooks.org

Library of Congress Cataloging-in-Publication Data
Names: Watson, Ellen, 1950- author.
Title: Pray me stay eager / Ellen Doré Watson.
Description: Farmington, ME : Alice James Books, 2018.
Identifiers: LCCN 2017021878 (print) | LCCN 2017026374 (ebook) | ISBN
9781938584732 (eBook) | ISBN 9781938584688 (paperback : alk. paper)
Subjects: | BISAC: POETRY / American / General.
Classification: LCC PS3573.A8523 (ebook) | LCC PS3573.A8523 A6 2018 (print) |
DDC 811/.54--dc23
LC record available at https://lccn.loc.gov/2017021878

Alice James Books gratefully acknowledges support from individual donors,
private foundations, the University of Maine at Farmington, the National
Endowment for the Arts, and the Amazon Literary Partnership.

Contents

≠

≠ *one* ≠

≠ *t w o* ≠

≠ *three* ≠

Acknowledgments

≠

I gratefully acknowledge the editors of the follow publications in which these poems, sometimes in different versions or under different titles, first appeared:

The Academy of American Poets' Poem-a-Day, "Thin Ice" (January 2016)

The American Poetry Review, "Ode to Abstractions" (Vol.41/No.1, Jan./Feb. 2017)

Barrow Street, "Field Guide to Abstractions" (Winter 2017/2018)

Birmingham Poetry Review, "One of the Waves" and "What We Carry" (#44, spring 2017)

Boulevard, "Lifeboats" (Nos. 95 & 96, spring 2017)

The Common (online), "Hungry Ghost" (May, 2017)

Copper Nickel, "March 31st and the Frogs" (#25, fall 2017)

Crazy Horse, "Hermitage" and "This Ledge I Live On" (spring 2018)

Diode, "The Animal with Irony" and "The Field Wants Its Sheep Back" (February 2017, 10TH Anniversary Issue)

Field, "Revel" (#96, spring 2017)

The Golden Shovel Anthology: New Poems Honoring Gwendolyn Brooks, "True & False" (University of Arkansas Press, 2017)

Green Mountains Review, "The Wonder" (online, fall 2017) and "Learning to Sail at 57 on Father's Day" (print, spring 2018)

Gulf Coast, "Word" and "How Many Nests of What" (Issue 30.1, October 2017)

The North (U.K.), "Amen," "Which Deep of Me," and "Things I Can't Explain" (#45, fall 2015)

Salamander, "No Ode" (#44)

Smartish Pace, "Some music" and "Too-Big November" (#24, April 2017)

Tampa Review, "Mother Going Gone" (#55, fall/winter 2017)

Zone 3, "April Eclogue" (fall 2011)

This book would not be what it is, without—

~ the crucial gifts of space/time/solitude/community/belief I found in the places & people of The MacDowell Colony, Yaddo, and The Hermitage;

~ the kind/stern/brilliant nurturing of my poetry family—Barbara Ras, Annie Boutelle, Amy Dryansky, Diana Gordon, Maya Janson, Mary A. Koncel, Carol Potter, Joan Houlihan & Abe Louise Young.

~ I'm also grateful to dear nourishing friends & colleagues at Smith College, *The Massachusetts Review*, the Drew University MFA in Poetry and Poetry in Translation, & Alice James Books (with special thanks to Carey Salerno).

~ I would not be the person/writer I am without the presence of Adélia Prado & Adelia Doré Moran in my life.

For my parents, Marion Doré Watson & Rev. James Charles Watson

1924 –2007   &   1919 –2015

Thrust / Thirst

Fan-fronds of latania palm—
their spray of many-fingered
many hands: *excitement* or *alarm*?

one

Message in a Bottle

Her desk sits plopped lonely but points
true north. Her sins: ingest, scorn,
postpone. She curses her good luck,

thinking to keep it. It's her birthday
but she'd rather her daughter's, three
days later and unregrettable. She feasts,

she festers. Hates partitions and in-
decision. Should she opt to be thrown
to the wind over earth or water?

She treasures ears full, ears empty.
Stone. Floating. Flame. She means
to destabilize her vanity, wrinkle

by roll. Bring your lust and you'll learn
her shame. Her finger points, her palms
cup. She gives and takes with both

hands. Frets, fritters, bolds. She's the dog
on the bone but doesn't wait well.
I am standing at the looking glass looking.

The Animal with Irony

I agreed to hold the snake just long enough
for my brother to wrestle the cage door open.

The cat who retracted her claws to tap my cheek
was the one who brought to the back stoop

the most carnage: star-nosed mole, cartoon
chipmunk, pumping-chested finch. I confess

to an alligator purse, my kid-fingers pressing
and yanking the ridged forehead to snap and

unsnap the snapper. In Brazil, a grisly still life
under flat sun: one eight-inch severed turtle leg,

one trembling flour sack tied tight, and José,
scared and purple with rage, bellowing at five

ragtag boys, bloody knives in their fists and
hungry. When an elephant hurls her dung,

it's time to handcuff the keeper. Whatever our
human cruelty, the existence of silverfish says

hell is not clean and alive like fire. Bless
the horse, ducking her head into the bridle.

Bless her neighborly whinny as I crest the drive.
Though it has cost me five cats and many chickens,

I live rural to be near wild. Chuff of bear. Coyotes'
nightly tune-ups thrill, swooningly jagged: perverse

reassurance I'm glad for. The hawk's Thanksgiving
arc-swoop, his talons' cursive, writ on our tiniest pullet,

spoke a savage grace. Infant scream of fisher, knock-
rattle in the night basement, these jitter me alert,

alarmed, which I take as gift, since fear conquered
equals pride—but is anything more suspect?

Less animal? We name and eat and love and loathe
them. On account of flowers, I no longer allow

groundhogs their cuteness, vote instead for Chuck's
gun. How tenderly I jar crickets and bumblebees,

deliver them to their outside lives, yet whack moths,
snip wasps with gusto, trap mice, lay poison for ants,

flush ladybugs down the toilet. Having once ordered
thousands to sprinkle about the garden, now

I celebrate as their masses dwindle and disappear
from ceilings and screens, returning me my kindness.

The Night Doesn't Summarize the Day

The day doesn't even speak to the night because
that would be like recognizing Palestine. Small doses
of darkness are permissible, light pretends to own
nothing, or everything. *Everything* is a trap.
Against the night, people pitch tents. Inside the tents,
we make of our skin lanterns. Look how skin and
lanterns in proximity evoke lampshades made of skin
—unspeakable!—and how this spawns settlements
and unpeaceable. How certainty solidifies the *we*,
but scours a body out. Joining a we that means to be
impermeable, we think only leaks and locks. Water-
boarded only in our sleep, we wake to find our armature
a hulking tilty thing squatting on the dirt, casting a loutish
shadow over something green and fixing to feel the light.

Field Guide to Abstractions

How to distinguish *faith* from *faithfulness* from
loyalty from *blindness*, or see the *hate* in *envy*?
Do you detect a difference between male
and female *generosity*? Field guides are by nature
particularly pebbled. *Practice* makes etcetera.
    But we can't draw *awe*,

so the usual maps and illustrations are out: no
Topography of *Misery*, no field marks of upper
and lower *sorrow*, no tricolor Range of Habitat,
nothing newsy like "The 'Cow Killer' (aka
'Velvet Ant') dwells in woodland edges—
    and is really a wasp."

So we commandeer birders' categories:
Aerialists (*risk*)
Long-legged waders (*adventure* & *hope*)
Raptors (*opportunism*)
Smaller waders (*helpfulness*)
Swimmers (*curiosity* & *gossip*)

Note: While the inside cover of *Birds of the Southeast* bears
a ruler, Abstractions will prove difficult to measure.

Ode to Pleasure

You come in the piquancy of ginger, of fingers,
the startle of clean teeth, the sight of a stigma
dusty with rusty pollen that makes for more
flowers and more bees. You're about noticing,
then submersion. But wisp, where do you live—

you more-than-comfort, you singular multitude,
shapeshifter, two-ticket ride, you sometime visitor
unwilling to move in? If you did, would you look
like a drug? *Just a teaspoon, please* will never cut it.
Oh, Pleasure, you flood us when we're doing well

what we love well—in the midst of you, you're all
there is—but you can be drilled out of existence by
time spent in solitary: six-by-nine-foot cinder block
cells that break brains. I didn't mean to turn dark.
In fact, you're sticky. Look—I'm already deserting

the ones we lock in boxes—because I'm in a place
conducive to pensiveness *and* dancing. And truly,
I meant to sing your simple praises, after seeing
that photograph and sitting in the conundrum
of ravishingly hurt hands, before the Malian music

flooded me back to you. Sometimes we woo you,
others you just sweep in. If only you scared me more.
Not minding my fingers going purple on the frigid
porch for the first cigarette in years equals danger.

But I gobble you up. You're a pear perfectly ripe,

you're the giving and the taking, a spontaneous
shoulder touch, belly laugh. You are running water
and the floating on it, you're natural selection:
our drive to sex—and clans. You're what's *found*
in translation, you live in the pirouette between

brain and body. And even now, you're skittering
away. Shadows fall on the page, on my skin,
unbidden tattoos that bid me talk tough: Why
the fuck are you so well-behaved? Elusive, fine,
but why not intrude where you're needed, slip

through the bars? If the definition of depression
is a door shut to you, blast it open, Pleasure,
why float above the fray? You're not just a noun,
you're a verb! No, something's wrong here.
We strike a match, share you around, breathe

your imagined breath, verby and herby with rush,
and forget that you are true but no truer than
the lack of you. You're as subjective as they come,
but—whether doing time or killing time—we're
the subject of the sentence, its human weight

and worry. A wise man said, *Don't look inside.*
Look outside and see what the inside does with it.
Those rivered hands. My eyes fill with them,
then fill. And I'm no longer talking to you, but
to myself: should I be permitted (this) pleasure?

If Dancing

Where dancing is forbidden, do people
sprout wings

Where does the mind go while we dance

What if dancing to the point of upthrust, downfall—

What if dancing while playing Ping-Pong, bathing,
while negotiating a turn

I'm tired of dancing with myself

What if my fingers danced up your spine

Dance of mica-shine, dance of epicenter—

What if that girl means to dance herself to splinters

What if ankle, calf, what if tibia and fibula

What if you want to be touched everywhere except
where the dancer's hands gravitate

What if your best friend's grief has pinned her
to the dance floor

And your father's dancing partner—

What if music didn't belong to everyone

Or someone said, *Dance*, while shooting at your feet

What if you see a photo of Cunningham's hands—
wings above his wheelchair

Mother Going Gone

Year after year you keep on being gone, gone
after years and years of gone, of marginal, mute,
vacant, of breathing, and then, within minutes, a shy
descent, some huffs and stutters, and a hushing
to waxen, no, to stone-gone, finally unloosed
(to our tired, to our relief) to revisit us—gleeful,
earnest, jigging *you*, who I wear on my left pinky,
on my worn face, all through the fading, the warm
forgettable grief, the still water of it, until my own
tides' tugging, morning's horror-mirror, rude singleton-
time, its skeletal, long view of the hurtling, the way
the body speaks of it, first one syllable then two, and you
still gone, and him here, ancient, healthy, walls of all-
he-is inching inward, leaving him small and dawdling.

April Eclogue

Damned forsythia—ramrod upthrust intent
on a head start! While we—greedy for color—
haul it into overdrive in overheated houses
and force it to make pretty, and the clump
outside flexes and plots to overtake
the pachysandra, upend the stepping-stone.
But so little is all *this* or *that*, dead mouse
stiff-crooked in the trap but oh! velvet gray.
The beech tree—guts bored from within, skin
freeze-fissured—a body-builder from the waist
up only, is over-stretching its arms, reaching
as if to the next county, as if to buy a few years.
You say we're all shameless with it—*ongoingness*.
I sigh, set my jaw, I mean to green into my wreckage.

Hungry Ghost

The Hungry Ghost is not the bakery on State Street
of the same name, but the toothy fire the baker

thinks he's tamed. At thirteen, a blast of lightning
levitated me, then bolted me to my bed until a fierce,

rhythmic flickering behind the blinds drew me up
to see the top half of Cindy's house—roaring.

In woods and alleys, kids strike matches, grab
danger. Once, I followed sirens to a big blaze,

posed as a novelist desperate to get it right. A guy
ducked me under the tape, handed me a hardhat,

let me close enough to sweat, small in the scalding
light. Thinking love combustion, we forget smolder,

go for conflagration. We get scorched, apply simple
salve, drink too little water. Don't we all fall silent,

enthralled, before woodstove or hearth or warming
our hands under the overpass, knowing only stone

and bone survive it? Fire, you made us who we are—
cooks, night owls, large-brained dreamers. Because

we can't take you into our bodies, we settle for smoke,
inching ever faster toward the red-tipped end. But

oh my people, when it's time, please. Give me
to the fire. Let it eat me, immaculate and gone.

How Many Nests of What

In a net of light against the buggy dusk,
squinting at my neighbor's just-hayed field,

hot whir still in my ears from the sicklebar
that wiped out how many nests of what, or

nearly? The wind—lately just a whisper-
brush on cymbals—rises fierce. Like Richter

with his I-beam, it scrapes a wide stain
across the fast-fading sky. A gift of pigment

to close a black-white day run through
by a late taste of blood. The article

I'm reading in seeming womb-light says
happiness is historically related to morality.

Stop to wonder whether happiness is instead
simply present or (zap!) gone—maple sap

by late April alive only in its sweet bottled
form—but *morality*? Whose? Maybe

it's something stupid simple as: give without
get. Extrapolate! And, get this, my thesaurus

says the opposite of happiness and virtue is
guilt—better known as internal bleeding—

which swivels me to the innocents: velour
of mouse or bird breast—and could one still

be heaving out in the close yonder? I eat flesh
and can't blame the farmer. Or my human dead,

forever bringing up my failings. Though maybe
they're forever changing like the sky in my eyes.

Too-Big November

1) A photograph: knotted rough-cut pine nearly all
this kitchen is. Silverware nailed to the wall, speaking
beauty only to our eyes. 2) Emma of a sudden cold
in the November ground, unfinished—a beauty just
last week in her kid brother's pants. 3) A mountain
of a man who says mind is a turn-on. These three
hugenesses my chest won't hold. I try turning them
on their heads. Forks and spoons rain their glow—
but Emma Rose—impossible—impossibly empty,
death is. There it sits. Stark as a kitchen that allows
no soft or sitting. Backs to scratchy barn-board,
they would have had to stand to eat. I am sorry
as water, then inexplicably as loose. How can he
call me *lovey?* Oh, I am silly with its return...

Field Guide to Abstractions

The naturalist says recognition is not seeing; seeing
leaves *judgment* home, asks questions. Why is *grief*
a towering cumulus? What are the characteristics
of this or that species of *defeat?* A doctor who treats

brain injuries watches a woodpecker, asks, *Why no
head trauma?* Learns the tongue serves as shock
absorber and the brain's not loose like ours. Some
moths disguise themselves as bird shit, bark. Look

at the fish. Look at the fish again. Let's see if this
works for *sanity. Elegance.* Choose your abstraction
and observe daily through the seasons, noting change
and pattern. *Despair* fades to *disquiet.* Look hard

at *humility.* Where there's water, there's fish, there's
osprey. If bitten, determine: by *fear* or *honesty?*
Keep calm. Timely administration of the right
serum insures the *possibility* of *recovery.* Look again.

Lifeboats

Morning radio chides a woman for wanting her dead
    hand cut off. Morning sidewalk displays
a frayed robin on its side, oh still-breathing eyeblink.
    The robin rights itself, wobbles, lists left, I
walk away. All day I scrap with money and machines,
    time trumping words, while knots needle softly
into deep aches—the forgotten body first peeking

    out, then chewing at the doorjamb, a dog who
just wants to be owned. That dusty robin was a heap
    of trying. The woman, too, begging for the knife,
certain it was time to cut the ballast free. Conventional
    but brave, my mother had no chance to choose.
Before she knew it, she was a pale turnip withering
    on the board. It made no sense to press soil gently

to her and water, but we did. Evening radio reminds me
    what I'm hankering to eat, and a wispy voice wonders,
Doesn't the body deserve its rest? (People make fusses to make
    hay.) A surgeon retorts: *Brain-dead donors are put on—*
not life but—organ support, and briefly. The soul is free to go.
    I order that dish with the ground chicken and lettuce
leaves, extra hoisin. I take the doc's side, whether or not

we have a soul. *Fund-raising is a little like barn-raising,*
says the next host as I take a long look at the bridge so close
   to breaking that within the week the long way around
will crowd my days like a deadline. I pick up the takeout, head
   home to do my taxes and despair of time. The river
glitters. I try to say thanks every chance I get. I vow to wash
   my hair, think: the robin must be a goner by now. Between

the trees naked fields stake their claim, blackbirds glean. Dusk
   is a half-open door into the dozen dialects of memory.
It's time to turn off the radio. My garage opens at the flick
   of a switch, thanks to my father, insister, installer.
Please god may his dog outlive him. For once the restaurant
   remembered the hoisin, though there are never enough
lettuce boats to lower gently onto the flat blue sea of my plate.

Amen

I believe in trees. Sun-stunned,
forking, house of shade and moan
and burning. I don't want a god who
bleeds, I want a shepherd to herd me
homewise, toward wood and stone
and making. Tomorrow is the place
we put what we're afraid of. Today,
lists. Give me a now where whispers
come bidden and unbidden, visions
follow. Give me belief not outward
but in—I want what's waiting to out.

Things I Can't Explain

Oboes. Boredom. The hole smack in my heart when
my parents were in the room. The heron who stands,
regal for hours three days in a row beside the surf-casting
couple, though they give him nothing. That they give him
nothing. The intractable one percent of anything. How one
boy can flee from brutal, while his brother ramps it up.
Why, when asked if he was a happy man, de Gaulle said,
What do you take me for, a simpleton? How dreams
dissolve, wet tissue. How the real. Why a green doorway
in a yellow house with a thigh-high pile of fresh-picked
coffee beans on the floor makes me cry. Why the woman
who owns the doorway can't walk through it. Why
she holds thumb to index finger—sign of a dove—
to hold the plane aloft. Why we're not on it when it falls.

Learning to Sail at 57 on Father's Day

My tiller arm is achy. I have a hard time overriding
instinct. He says pick a landmark if the wind is confusing.
Having said that is a phrase I like. The water: froth
on navy-gray marble but churning liquid. I think
"l" sounds. He says the sea is forgiving. Or is it the wind?

He says make smaller adjustments. I made pan-seared salmon
and couscous, which got cold as he took a call from the first-
born. Yesterday's scripture was the Prodigal Son. I put on
the good brother's robe of resentment. He labels each
leftover. The kitchen table is older than I am. Good little

brother told me steering by land is just boating—to sail
you have to get the hang of the wind. It's only too late
for something if you decide it is, and I do. We're tacking
back now, which means the long way, with lots of angles.
Later, we'll take a drive in the hybrid. A fox will dart out

from lawn of luxury to seaside scrub—and as soon as
I think this in words, it will enlarge. Dad is our cranky
centerboard in his ratty rubber boots. The ocean's new
cut-through threatens houses belonging to millionaires,
of which there are many. But so much there is that can't

be owned. Little brother is almost taken out by a truck,
whether or not the Lord had anything to do with almost.
Or with the sun's red rise the next morning. Our father
who art in Chatham releases the dinghy, shakes the sand
out of the lock, and leans into the long drag toward the tide line.

Needing Away

At waking, weightlessness mists off, we're embodied,
fog turned to lava. Yellow is about to discover itself

and write the sun's summons. Dark to glow to daily.
I leave soft and creamy for hard-bodied and hurtling,

I leave auto for pilot, as if in charge. Officer, charge me.
I'm lurching, reeling in the road like a too-big fish,

as if what I'll do when I get to do it matters. Where
has the flannel of me gone? The low-down, the float?

Newspeak like hardened wax-words in my ears—
not all for naught: petitions to sign, cauldrons

of cares worth caring. But in the midst, I need lilt,
I need away. Flick a switch: 100 women's voices—

Zimbabwe surround sound, serious honey backed by
drilling drums, and I'm in Harare, free and sheepish,

accepting the flash-fried *macimbi* worm into my mouth
and forgiven for regretting it as soon as crisp gives way

to goo, after the goat, the toasts, after the real and ritual
handwashing, after the dust-blown boulevard flanked

by flame lilies, poisonous, sexy, protected—lily-poachers
sell them, 8 bucks a bouquet roadside, blazing, illegal.

Before bed, let the speeding ticket, botched omelet,
locked horns drop off the day's ledge, swim instead

in its top 3 moments: lushness beaming me up, the one
true word ratified by eyes, the going out on a limb

that tickled. To think that remembering triggers physical
change in the brain, that brain is body, and all it holds

wisps away when we go—but when only shadow-gone,
delivered to drifting, to unlawful, uncaged—flying to sleep,

our day-selves slink off like predators yawning home.

Field Guide to Abstractions

Plump like a starling or slender like a cuckoo?
Deeply forked, square-tipped, notched, rounded, or pointed?
Fine like a warbler's, stout like a sparrow's, daggered like a tern's,
    or hook-tipped?
Do you note mustache stripe, eye-rings, or wing bars?
Does it spiral up treetrunks or jerk down headfirst?
Does it glide or soar?
Undulate like a flicker, fly straight like a dove, hover like a
    kingfisher?
Does it cock its tail or not?
Dive deepwater or dabble and upend?
Probe the mud or teeter and bob?
Ask these questions of your *love/jealousy/loneliness.*

t w o

$$\neq \quad \neq$$

Hermitage

Hard to the left of the house, the path,
the footbridge, the way back. To her
back, the Gulf. The only woman
among busy men now gone
to martinis, missing out on sleeves
of clouds, the shapes they fashion
to frame stars. She was none of these,
woman man cloud star. Maybe more
gulf or sleeve. *Woman of a certain
age* means—how old. Well beyond
the middle. Taking this in would take
muscle. But how to leave the wild
wet edge, the shushing at her heels.
Not true. She was already sitting
on the splintery bridge, struck
by creature-noise in those flat
clattery leaves, almost friendly.
This is not strictly a story. I left
her longer on the beach than she
dared, and the bridge was not
where she stopped in the soft
whiffle of air but at the window
of the house, looking in, where
she was also, waiting. To know
some things. Which I will never tell.

Ode to Abstractions

Because we can't touch or taste ghosts but we
sense them. Because abstract or not: *adoration,*
sacrifice—many someones are surely intimately

inside them now. Because signifiers, even though
amorphous. Because amorphous can be solace
to the single. Believe me. Because alone, low,

lowing. The teacher says, *We all communicate*
with abstractions at times... (Picture 4th-graders
working up steam, trying to address *courage*

or *deceit)...but abstract nouns can't convey things*
we experience with our senses. Wrong! Say *fear*
and my stomach plummets. On cue, a tangible raccoon

ambles toward the open bulkhead and I convey
displeasure, loudly. Let's say I become a banshee.
O the outside inside. O peripheral vision. He wants

to move in, to paw specific jars of tomato sauce
off my pantry shelf onto the cellar's cement like
last year. Teacher says, *Abstract words mean*

different things to different people, which I find
comforting. The daylilies are impervious. The ones
impossible to uproot, leggy and common, like those

my ex and I picked in this same muggy rain just
before our wedding forty years gone, but that's
not why I disprize them. They have exactly nada

to do with *betrayal*. Because *time*. Because trees
whose branches fling down instead of thrusting up
are no more sad than my eyes make them. Because

today instead of descending fireworks, my neighbor's
willow is *hope*—a tired and trusty skeleton subject
to gravity that yet carries us, carries us. Do the right

thing, children. Take those abstractions and chew
them. Because digestive juices. Up down sideways,
take *barbarity* between your teeth, suck awhile on *mercy*,

let *curiosity* populate your gut. Because *idiosyncrasy*
is a species of brave *vagrancy*, volunteer *singledom*,
because O dear hearts, *now* is ours—and genuine

laughter, even for no reason, is no, never abstract.

LAX to BDL

Fishing for my fallen purse, I grab the fine pointy-toed
caramel leather peeking out from under my seat, feel
a powerful urge to caress it, and wonder how the guy

in 12D with the foot in that shoe would react. It doesn't
help that I've already noticed: nice cut of suit, right amount
of wrinkles, no wedding band—and he's kneeing my back

gently through the seat. Returning from the loo, I think:
walk up, lean down, plant a brief kiss on his cheek (or
mouth, depending). Say, *So nice to see you.* To be clear,

I only see us with all our clothes on—real lust lately
gone underground from lack of habit and hope. Dear
Mr. Caramel, how about we start with a meaningful

look, delicate iron filings lining up to posit true north—
of the exploratory sort. What's gotten into me? My married
friends' concern—or their own extracurricular longings?

To the one who asks, *Have you ever considered…you know,
women?* I say yes—but no: I want to be the (only) one
with breasts. And now we're beginning our slow descent,

me, my friends, the plane and Mr. C. , who's up for a last
pee. Waiting for his stroll back, I consider sticking out a foot
to trip him, playful, purposeful. Here goes—but look, he took

his glasses off and his face got longer. My foot stays where
it is and I do nothing to catch his gaze. Such a chickenshit.
Remember in the movies, thigh to thigh with an appealing

stranger for hours, me struck dumb, not even a stray comment
as the lights came up. I hang back as we deplane, and here he
comes, looking rumpled, sluggish, kind of watery, just like me.

Numbers

≠ First, I have only one rule: face front.

≠ Secondly, I lied.

≠ Besides, 2 is my—well, right now my least favorite #.

≠ Though it has been pleasurable several many times.

≠ Two can be really-fine, really-fine, fractious, fractured, finis.

≠ Do platonics and occasionals count?

≠ We won't speak of their quality or #s, which I have
no desire to reconstruct. No *desire*, really—of that sort.

≠ Lie #2 (what I just said).

≠ What I mean is, I'm single but I've never played so much
music.

≠ Many gods is more confusing than one, but maybe that's
for the best?

≠ The man talking about the discovery of zero lost me.

≠ Well, to be fair, I was distracted—in one of my favorite
ways. You know, when qualitative and quantitative
converge.

≠ Why does the photo of three horses in the field
pierce me more deeply than the ones and twos?

≠ The power of three—sheets to the wind, blind mice, BLTs,
French horns, stooges, the # of bones in the human ear.

≠ Still lifes: how many nouny-things are required to create
pungency?

≠ I seem to be avoiding big #s.

≠ How many is too many: choices, vices, ladybugs, heroes?

≠ Whatever money is, there are many grubby digits in it.

≠ Casualties, too. Too many and counting…

≠ …vs. countless laughs if we're lucky.

≠ Infinite?—oh, pishposh. Let it go.

≠ I admit for a time I watched *One Life to Live*, and it's true.

≠ Finite. Finito.

≠ Rule #2: I have three life-or-death requirements:

≠ The first knows her name,

≠ The second's what I'm doing,

≠ And the third—leave me with at least three out of five senses.

≠ Admittedly, for x # of years, touch has been let us say subtle.

≠ And while (a minimum of five sprigs of) lilac equals intoxicating—perhaps not as utterly as the other three.

≠ Fuck, I refuse to choose between the last ones.

≠ Is this universal?

≠ What about memory? How much would I trade for more now?

≠ Right now, one browning leaf falls onto the piano, which remains silent.

≠ I admire them equally (doing what they must), and think to turn on the radio.

≠ Rule #3: sideways has its merits.

≠ *Will I disappoint my future if I stay?* asks breathy Sade.

≠ Me, I'd change the verb to *go*.

≠ For the *nth* time, *Yes*.

≠ And one more thing. Whichever end of the spectrum,

≠ There's no # for how I feel.

True & False

Creatures don't experience simultaneous eager and
unready. Does the swift tawny gazelle even *know* eager, if
she's a gazelle—not a woman who craves savanna and sun,
or thinks she does, despite inner-unraveled, need for dark. Comes
first hint of light, she tunnels under, insists night linger, wonders
    how
ever to shine, wonder undermining, head hammering: how shall
I approach tender tenderly, ever—much less tiptoe toward *we*,
when bare means naked means fear, means no means to greet.
Despite deep flutter, she means—true & false—to meet him.

March 31st and the Frogs

are going nutso down in that sinkhole
pond. Sounds like a cauldron on high
happy boil. I'm not there yet, you're
nonexistent, my roommates are vices.
All that I read confirms darkness—who
asked poems to be lugubrious chariots
to the pitch? It's safe, though, living
in paper rooms with words arriving
oh yes like bullets, expected, or like
manatees—wonder underwater.
Those actual frogs are nothing but
out there, with their three-chambered
nonhuman hearts, their skin cleaning
the air we share, and they could care
less whether I thank or curse them
for their farty calls speaking sex.

Eyes bat open to dog-yips

and big window shock of blue. I breathe thin dry air,
foreign in sun-blasted mesa while time zones away
a great storm approaches. People are filling their tubs
and charging everything electric. Landfall they call
what happens next, water slamming the edges of
everywhere. My shopworn rickety cat salivas her fur,
then nips it out in wads, alone hours and days
in the whipped house. A muddy rush of cellar-river
flushes the resident woodchuck to higher ground.
Punky sodden roof-fascia release their iron jewelry,
drowning furnace and fridge-hum. Water coughs,
then stills in the well. The welling in me hangs fire.
I lean east and listen, fresh from learning that hearing
is the last sense to desert us as we take our leave.

My heart is in no way first,

does not fly, is neither free nor bound, fastened only
to my daughter and my chest. If this sounds like a riddle,
it is. See how I make light—while this moving part throbs
in its shadow-cave, desperate to be the body's window.
Far off, my tree shivers its siren call. I can't make out
what I long for. Praise longing, it's what keeps us un-
finished (not undone). Singing wholes me while its ache
thrums hunger. I'm not asking for the air to be strangely
stirred, much less for the world to bemoan my lack
of a fellow porter in this late life. Dean Young, newly
be-hearted, claimed poems are not about making cages,
but birds. Give me this bready day the piece of me
I know least. The raspy one that puts the body's valentine
on vibrate and rustles up another on-the-wing song.

Hearing Aids

We laugh as he squiggles them into his ears,
the pink plastic of Barbies, but my friend is not

pleased: *So, this is what I get? For a couple thousand
bucks, a parakeet turns into a crow?* Fishing, I ask,

What about (he would die without) *music?*—but
no, his beloved *fado* sounds like the dishwasher.

And oh, did I say my friend is in love? *At my age?
Am I crazy?* he asks. Maybe, but he deserves her

—*and* to hear! Maybe we'll never again be the selves
we remember, but isn't complication fun? (My dad's

complication at ninety-one: seven-man Friday lunch
finally reduced to: him.) I tell my stricken friend we

could have twenty-plus years left—who knows
the wonders to come of our rack and ruin?

After all, you said, *Peeing sounds like shards of glass
crashing onto the tin roof of the water in the bowl.*

This Ledge I Live On

As night shoulders down around, still
there is weedbed, crabapple, doorjamb,
light pouring onto grass-shiver. Lamp
by room I darken the house, like a body
easing without fight into dying. Step out,
sit in the sandpile under the copper beech.
Distant lit boxes blink off. No moon.
The treeline stays friendly. It's never been
the sky that threatens, but humandark,
hearsay, newsprint—the dice. Shake them
out onto the flagstones. Something brutal
may once have happened on this modest
hill. Surely this ground has felt the weight
of falling bodies, this ledge seen grief. If
you can predict the next when and what,
don't. Leave me unknowing in the delicious
dark, here where fear's as out of place
as yesterday's three chickens strutting
Route 116, more silly than unsafe.

Ode to Fear

When I say *fear*, I'm not talking humiliation-
anxiety, no, not even mortal fear—I mean
the *abyss*. And it's not just the reaper I refuse,
but his vestibule. That we're given no X
on the calendar, no vaccine for the waiting—

and not just what waits for me, or the clouded
plaque prior, but for you, oh daughter—delivered
of my body. I known this isn't much of a praise
song, but here we are, love, or will be. Behold
the inviting expanse of biting white snow,

ravishing too-muchness tainted by a stab of fear.
So much death lies ahead. Can I say that?
A long series of swallowings. And the studded club
of a word, two syllables snaking on the wind,
threatening blackout in my brain circuitry: *outlive*.

Last night you thanked me for teaching your child-self
not to suffer in advance. Fear, the great obliterator
of now. Grace, the not letting it. So where's the 10-blade,
clean and lethal, to slice *out* from *live*? (Stay with me,
I say to me. Try to not be gone—and not just

not until you're gone—for every ever.) Fuck fear.
This ode is to the knife of wind, the blowing snow,
the why I walk into the cold quieted world, so vast
and silent I hear my heartbeat and believe that you
will lay me down (can I say that?) one day.

All I Can Think of Is the Assault Weapon in Some Someone's Hands

All   ready.
I   try thinking elsewhere, otherwise, anyplace.
Can   not, not today.
Think   of huge clips of ammo I don't know the words
               for, the reason,
Of   the brainfold where a videogame-glorygroove
               dreams real.
Is   on its way to.
The   day of reckoning, wrack, eradication nation.
Assault   is the opposite of salt, wit, zest, keep.
Weapon   and assault sound ludicrously clean.
In   words.
Some   deeds bleed the words from our mouths.
Someone's   scarred shuck of a boy, stuck in the bloody
               comeuppance he holds in his
Hands.

Last Night Late

I pushed an accosting man down,
down, flat-backed, and fist-
pounded his sternum,
a long-dormant EMT gesture
gone wrong on purpose—
but of course this is a tale.
Brother Black Belt surely
would say: *Only if his center
of gravity was off.* Well,
he was squirrely and we were
in a suburbia of inanimate
objects, not a pound of flesh
visible but for this polo-shirted,
flare-eyed lost one. I wonder,
what if I had had a knife?

It Began with the Ping-Pong Balls

Syrian activists scritching *freedom* on thousands
of them, rolling them down cobbled streets to amaze
and embolden, tossing them into a nest of sleeping

soldiers to bounce wildly: click-clocking mockery,
impossible targets, while Stateside, at the Presbyterian
Home, residents document their lives: here they are

on YouTube in a box beside an Egyptian blogger posting
nude photos of herself *to break taboos*—and is she
brave or foolish?—while white smoke gives us the first

Jesuit Pope and I flip from irate—such hyped suspense
—to elated: he wears regular shoes! The Syrian rebels
dump red food coloring into the town square's fountains,

waffling me from *Wish them luck* to *Someone has got to save
these people.* Oh, no, wait—that was 2011, two years
ago. Now their M.O. is to dance at funerals, and how many

more are left? No one I know has had to choose to endanger
or not to endanger their family. Meanwhile, I surf:
Laos looks a lot like the D.R. except for the roofs, curly

upside-down V's, and I'd like to taste those fish on sticks
and that waterfall is a doppelganger for one Lewis and Clark
visited in Oregon. Me, too. But it's not landscape, it's stories

that keep me at the keyboard: Frank Schubert, lighthouse
keeper. Cali Rivera, cowbell maker. Bernard Greenhouse,
"A Master and His Cello," who shows us the difference between

technique and expression, three hundred-year-old wood
put to excruciating millisecond delays, deep vibrato that says
there are things worth holding onto. Avoiding goofy dogs

and grand brunches posted by people I actually know, I dart
back to those Syrians who win my heart again, episode after
episode of *Top Goon*—finger puppet al-Assad pointy-nosed

in balsa wood, sidesplitting, devastating. Ashamed, I can't want
for a moment another war, but which to disavow—the shame
or the wanting? I cannot but let Bernard Greenhouse seduce me

to how *you know you're cooking if you feel it in your skin*. Ninety-
two,
he says he's fighting *the closure of his ability*—and he's not
going to let that happen, and I buy it, and we're both fools,

though I love him for it—but wait, this interview is dated 2008,
Bernard died in 2011, the year of the food coloring. Everything
connected and so disconnected—today (which will soon be

yesterday) it's: were chemical weapons used or no, and by who,
and will we know in time? I know nothing. Is it wrong to look
not for progress but containment, a la Bernard, whether it's

bowing ability or encroachment of evil? I know the beauty

human hands can make matters, but what to do about Syria?
Today's the first day of spring, hunger-time among the Puritans

I was trying to make poems of before booting up. Ten miles
and three centuries from here: root cellar bare, green shoots
just dream, blood and flame mere months away—no less

desperate than the head-scarfed girl on YouTube right now
in her careful English: *Save us, please.* Art and mayhem live.
How is it I can sigh, close the laptop, make myself a salad?

You Know What You Want and How Old Your Eggs Are

So go to him, the one who loves you more
than the one you love more, the one who wants
you wet or dry and not just Tuesdays, wants you
with every bit of his heart but for the purplish
corner that says his must be the design, and one
with no baby in it. Tell him no fluff. No bluff.
Bring Picasso into the room. Tell this man his roar
can be broken down into sex and sex and lullaby.
Put a flat warm stone in his palm, close his fingers
around it. Stand toe to toe and wash his body
with your eyes, then make of them a big enough
cradle. Ask: *Are we over or have we begun?*

What We Carry

Her arms ache as if from holding boulders, and I say,
It's your brother, the way you haul him around with you,
aware alternating with un-. At the end, he was all frame,
startlingly slight but full in his sudden leave-taking,
a hugeness she might have borne—if not for the mother-
ghost three years in her arms, murmuring, *No, not Mike,*
too. Empty-handed, I wonder back to how the long-sought
baby placed on my chest could so wholly eclipse the almost
ones, even Zeke who had a name. How otherwise: so herself,
our everyday wonder. But why, after years of mothering
this entire, does my own gone mother lie so lightly in my lap.
Why when it comes to Dad do I think duty, debt. Looping
questions undeserving of question marks—these are what I
stumble under—holding out, instead of holding out my arms.

Soul Sister Sonnet: Poet to Poet

When you call, you're living in the dark
of your throat. You hear nothing but ancient
machinery, iron-dry. I say what you'd say:
You've got the oil. If I were the one in the cave,
you'd say: *Roll away the stone. Even without*
the luxury of speech, press into what's next.
It's lonely without you, incomplete. If I said, Look—
garnets underfoot cutting facets in my feet,
Gather them, you'd tell me. *Love the bloody*
tracks you leave. Listen, sister: You will leave
the chafing-chamber and climb the ladder
to your teeth. Vocal cords are plural. I say
this today, you tomorrow: *Leave hollow,*
love fallow, be silo, words follow.

She draws crowds or fire. An oak, she towers.
She forewarns, she floors, she's sieve, she's oars
—all whirl and brimming—living for the world.
She's 13, first in her family to say *AIDS* out loud.
She's mopping nuclear meltdown at 69. She sun-
screens orphaned elephants' ears—knows mother
is shade. Thick-armed or reedy, she splits atoms,
invents windshield wipers, white out. She labors
in the bush the hut the tub the ward. She delivers.
Exponentially. She sisters. She gives us Hospice,
Kevlar, the Mars Rover, the bra. Carriers of water,
keepers of memories or bees. At 10, circumcised,
about to be wed, she spills hot tea in his lap, grows up
to write her memoir from jail—with eyeliner on t.p.
She will not be forbidden the world. Game-changers,
gene-mappers, those who build bridges, who *are* bridges,
who get the story told. Sharp- or honey-tongued, she
legals, loyals, triages, stops the superhighway. She sings
herself, and everyone. Flecked with paint or pain, knee-
deep in the way out or in. She drives. We women—elected,
reflecting, dissecting, refracting—ignition for the world.

Ode to Ologies

I'm glad there are people gleefully studying
the nature of knowledge and how it happens,
glad, too, there are judges of heart, of logic,
right and wrong action. The language starts
highfalutin, but boils down. You could say,
That's an ontological question or, *What's real?*
Add a personal POV and you've got phenomen-
ology—my favorite: *what is* filtered through
context and ache: a red handprint on a cave wall.

three

≠ ≠ ≠

The Field Wants Its Sheep Back

Of course that's me talking, but why wouldn't
it want a tickle of hooves, a warming of shit,
less empty? Sheep with their panoramic vision

are stressed by isolation, and sometimes
given mirrors, which comfort. Alone
can be expansive—balm or terror. Cold

is plural, swoop-seeps into the crowd
of everything else that is. (The Victorians
spent fully half their time trying to get

warm. Nowadays, only the poor, the jailed.)
Granted the lux of hearth or heat, frigid
is simply a slap, a tightening, survivable.

Cold is no shroud, but a reawakening,
the way the death of a friend of a friend
enlivens after it saddens. *Come no closer,*

says my every soggy cell. Cost costs.
Still-greenish tufts offer themselves up
all the way to the treeline. Despite

summer's sheep, they slowly whiten.
Let me spend wisely what I have,
which is only my breath—thin, visible

body heat. I am but a small animal.

Thin Ice

Reedy striations don't occlude the beneath—
earthy mash of leaves, flat pepper flakes, layered,

tips protruding, tender-desolate above a mirror
surface, gently pressing on horse-mane, nest material,

tickle-brush, fringe. Buff block-shapes further down,
ghost-bits of green-green, a lone leaf burned white.

My thrown stone skitters on ice. The next, larger,
plunks through, and for a moment I am a violator

but then I see that it opened a bubble cell, a city,
a lesion, a map—the way in cold and luminous.

Choices We Live With

Surf blooms out of breaking water, ragged rows
of dangerous blossoms. I'm inside a wave looking
for up—and out of nowhere your face beside me.
Pounding, spiraling, I am smiling, needles of water
up my nose a sure sign I am alive, and you a distraction
still. I give you up for kelp, a tricky handhold. Flat,
and slick, it gives way. Tumbled by another curl,
I scrape bottom, then cork toward light. Later,
on the beach, skinned places sting like new
loss. Without your hands, my chest rises and falls.

Not a Thing

I haven't been known   to address the Lord   expletives
                notwithstanding

Day by night   it's a human wow I'm after   the shiver-spank
  of a Zulu choir   suddenly in my car
                ceremony   that can't be summarized

When   night and day touch   they are neither one
    They ask of us nothing

Lacking an addressee   I do not   lack   wishes
    May M.'s rogue cells   in Rhode Island
                diminish   not crescendo

  How about less bereft all around

        but *bereft*   beautiful word   is off-limits
                my having been there   so seldom
    usually   nothing but   me-me-me   in my way

while for decades   R. has been moving his and others' kites
  and trains around   with his dark mind
                despite the odds

Ditto many   wondrous   others
    heavily laden   who still find the right
                verb   the right time
                        to burrow spark wade

Bless the quiet that can't   be stilled   Grant us
    if not completion   at least open   eyes
        Grant Y.'s   liver   the golden thread   its weaving

Give us glimpses   whiffs   of gone lives   and order
    the good kind   blooming in hot spots   Let

        my windows   clap softly open
             my hoarse   psalm twine

  Pray me stay eager

I'm stuck   on how foodie   and foodless
    don't touch

And how long will oil   matter more than water

   And how fast will plaque grow   into which
                  and whose   crevices

Relentless   week-long   rain
   pisses me off   one minute
       thrums me clean   the next

while elsewhere   walls and walls of it
      or none

  To do   unto   not to

Must I decide   to be alone   *not* to be

    For I haven't yet   learned   to address the sky
      and the verb to fathom   may never happen

but maybe a   lightbulb   is not   what we need
    For we are all   and each   on a train
      of whatever duration
          Before mine derails   why not ask

    Give us this day
      For the one right now   swallowed   by bereft
I ask
    for her   for   all of us

      I ask
        for   this thing   not a thing

astonishment

Barefoot Girl

for Adélia Prado

She climbed a tree to be noticed
by the singer but remained
invisible in the leaves. Not even
a basket in her yellow house
to turn onions and tomatoes
to beauty. Ten years later she
knew—yes, even withered: *still*
life. Sixty years later, she's still
terrified of (even rubber) snakes.
Not just water in her married house,
but electric hot. Appliances, Bibles,
many locks. Zé drawing griffins,
and fiddling with his ozone machine.
Mornings many sisters come to hail
Mary. Today the long noon table
welcomes grandkids who yearn to fly
this dusty city, and the radio lady
here to record our stroll down
to the barefoot girl's yellow house,
mere feet from the tracks where
a train, as if summoned, roars slowly
by, throbbing us from outside in.
Papa said we shake but don't fall.
Whose last days, whose feet rubbed,

That's the very tree, and always
in her side the three lifelong
thorns—*sex, death, God*—
that deliver without warning
fear, paintings, poems
we are helpless to refuse.

Revel

Apparently my house which wasn't my house was crumbling,
just like my real house is, in places. And under the ratty gold
carpet (which I would never tolerate), the floor was glass.
Somehow I stuck three fingers through a cut-through: waft
of cellar-air. Which room of me was that, to not go down into?
The answer came days later when my back went waffly
and lit a fire-strip down my right leg. I must need sistering,
like the rotten joists under the squeegee subfloor under
the punky linoleum tiles under the toilet. Meantime the only
valentine I got this year was an apology, and now here comes
that graying Scottie-dog and how much is left on my body's
mortgage? When the Mohawk dream a thing, they must do it.
Get baptized, go scalping. What about last week, the rifle shot
to the groin in of all places an elevator? And all I could think,
bleeding out, was some of us would name the shooter Vito,
others Otto or Muhammed. *Reap while you sleep*, said the ad
for collecting hotel points. Quelle harvest. I need a higher
power. Someone to push me around, whisper-deliver
the right command right in my ageless ear—*Revel! Revel!*—
so I wake with a mission—that's what I'd call reaping in sleep.

for Jean Valentine who does

One of the Waves

The tree guy said it would cost eleven hundred dollars to save
my two beeches and one crab. He looked like Robert Hass,
which sealed the deal. Ko Un said experience is not a mound
of fertilizer; what you learn should become part of your body.
Plow Guy invaded the flowerbed with gravel, and his son,

Lawn Guy, returned every bit to the driveway—I don't know
how but paid happy. Ko Un's wife said when he was released
from prison he was barely a cloud. Trees are our breathing,
but weak roots plus wind plus water equals *tim-ber*. I fret
whether the hemlocks should go, and the more precipitous

white pine. Tonight three hundred people inhaled Ko Un's
poems, proving that translation is rebirth. I'd like a late-life
sexual surprise like the of-a-sudden dusty Christmas cactus's
shenanigans last year. Tree Guy, a shorter, rougher Hass, wears
no wedding ring but does not do email. Ko Un shamed his
    captors,

filling his belly after each torture session, when they could not.
He says poetry says, *Have me!* but also that he writes not to
remember but to forget—sounding a little like my ex, but in no
other way do they resemble one another. This morning I broke
the bowl I made, beyond gluing. We must not whisper, whimper,

go walleyed. Says me. If my mother were alive she would kiss
these trees home and if my father could scale a ladder he'd help

take the weak ones down, down, down. After three suicide tries
over decades, Ko Un read of a monk's immolation and was
shamed. He stepped back from the boat railing, and now walks

the world as though his history weighs exactly zero. It's five
    years
since his visit, and the beeches, broken-backed with snow, must
be chopped. Ko Un would see no lesson, so I'm trying not to
    look.
I'm testing out his humble, his gusto, remembering his response
to my stammered, extravagant praise: *I am only one of the waves.*

Why Only Once This Dream

Even a soul submerged in sleep is hard at work.
—HERACLITUS

You're frozen at the back door. Cow-belly
planes swoop, roar, low-sweep the field.
Bomblets plop, sending up splinters
of things. A dull thud, then a hissing
in the stand of cherries, and you wonder
why *famously poisonous to cows* rings in your
ears just before the blast, its echo, and after,
dust breathing upward but not one thing
out of place. Your cell says you have a text,
tinkling on the table, silly. You follow
thwap-clatter to the window. A chopper
hover-lowers, the yard whipped, willow
shredded. This strikes you as personal.
You blunder out the front door, roll
down the lawn—elbows-to-hips, arms
cross-chested—like on TV, crash-land
in briars and blossoms. Your house is
you, is a ship at anchor, you don't know
which is listing, and today there's someone
ready to hack the rope. Your ivy-swamped
stoop has black lace-up shoes on it. Beside
the Christmas tree browning six months
in its stand stands a man. Is that your phone
in his hand? He surveys you, not bothering
to show his gun. Nine years later—and still you
worry: have you done enough to be the enemy?

The Wonder

We're sitting idle, another day of no skin,
no face up-turned. It's not that rain streams us

featureless, but there are bowls and there are
bowls, and our faces yearn to hold light. Meanwhile

the bright world, yellow and blue and crooked,
puts on a show of eternal, though we know

better. We're stuck with ourselves, and whatever
unseen hand holds the stopwatch. The wonder is

that suddenly one of us notices the merciful rounded
stones, another the silent *I was here* song of slugs,

another the sky invisible and elastic in the sound
of a siren. That self-disgust can get swallowed

by careful woodworking, tiny stitches, tickle and shine.
In the brush, in the mud, on the strut—so many

singers! We're all just squatters, but our gifts—
oh ears throat eyes fingers—extravagant.

Some music

fills me to the edges   chest of bright air   jaw
loosened   sometimes I imagine the makers   how
do they manage the flood size roundness   playing
impeccably on like that   gods they are   and I'm half
in love with a cellist I was in the same room with
half a day two years ago   the house creaking from sun
and settling   the cellist bowing for just three of us
and one asked   *can you make that riff sound*
like a question   and he did this cellist   and surely
I am much his elder   and how could I abide his rusty
stubble his untied untidy shoes   except when he's bent
to the work he calls play   and I didn't even love him then
though I wanted to *be* the cello   it's weeks later
and ever after in the car   push a button and his strings
vibrate   amber soaring through me   clothes loosening
so that whoever I think of is naked   sometimes
it's him   sometimes the current *possible*   or
I'm alone   but always the middle of me moist
and capable   and whatever rises up out of me
each time whatever proportion of bitter to sweet
swells full-bore toward that good kind of tears
and the drummy day or jetty night is blown
oh thank you wholly open

Which Deep of Me

I've been married longer to this house
        than to my ex. The clapboards may be
turning to mush, but the stars are out
        in force, and now and then I feel complete

in my hobbled way. With distressing
        irregularity, men walk my direction,
and undo me. I vow to remain clothed
        but unbound, ha-ha, as if I could, as if

it mattered. Appropriately ruined
        for my age, still I'd like not to be done
with *smitten*, the kind that flows both
        ways—we could have nothing

in common but elephants and hearts
        of palm and a partially open door.
The widower I truly can't wish a widower
        (whoever he is) might well

if I found him know how to love.
        Whether he would stay
depends on which womanparts
        he needs, which deep of me.

Ode to Edgelessness

Before time zones and property lines,
the world stood uncarved. Oh border
guards, oh flags planted on far planets,
oh confederacy of fences,
                              tops studded
with shards. Our forebears, prideful
to be non-scalping non-savages, flayed
this continent, and maps have always
been about owning.
                        Now we've got war-
toys that negate borders, zooming in
to peep or pinpoint. Trees, too, refuse
to stay in line: fir and spruce putting
the squeeze on quaking aspen,
                              but look
up at that hillside (for a while at least) all
shine and flutter—a rubbing of elbows.
We have neurons whose mission it is
to spot boundaries.
                        And what is love but
us smudging edges, mad to rub them out
and make with our two sticks one fire?
When jealousy (his) and inattention (mine)
drove a spike between us,
                              he resolved never
to look back. Some crossings diminish us;
others preserve the membrane (hopefully
permeable) that keeps us entire. How then

to get a handle on
    God,
who has no edges? Some leap to believe, leap
to safety, choose to cleave to (what I mostly see
as) cirrus; others take the land route, trusting
the human smooth—
        friendly breakups, good
deaths, strong handshakes, oh beauty,
palpable. But what of the fuzzy, edgy moments
sleep and waking touch, when we briefly
see another self,
     the inverted world
before it fizzles: a voice pebbled
with details streaming into my ear
things I need to know, and know
will not survive
     the trip back.
Invisibly attentive self stays sprawled,
listening, as the rest of me thirsts
upward, into this room, to wake,
thinking: *What*
    emergency have I lost?

Salad for Christmas

Satisfied? he asked, joke and acid in his voice,
and I stared at him, at the table, the faces around it,
the takeout containers empty of all but iceberg lettuce,
everyone but him bossed around and short on protein,
and remembered the last time I'd hurled scorn
back at my aged father. I am so provoke-able.
Cutting words feel good till the mouth snaps shut.
At first, less than half of me wants to scoop them back,
then the rest comes along. This ornery man is who he is
because of the iron he bequeathed me, and who am I
without it? How refuse him these moments of faux mastery,
barely enough to live on, what with his commode, his
daily succession of aides emptying it, his long love long gone
and his dog threatening to die before his body figures out how.
In two weeks I'll surprise myself, turning a ridiculous
round number. Hard enough from here to say, *When it's coming,
let it come*—imagine standing in a walker at the abyss?
Imagine leaning down to meet it, or scrambling
backward for whatever brief reprieve. There I am,
a cartoon figure grasping at roots, slamming down the cliff
in stages. Note to self: *walk a mile*—whenever you can.
And think *in his moccasins* instead of mocking.

The What

I walk out on morning feet
over the mole kingdom I like
a little better using that word,
despite their leavings in the stiff-
whitened grass: tall cow pie
constructions I imagine packing
gently, clay-cold and earthy,
on your back, night by night
attacked by fire, the kind only
hands and upright can quench,
oh your big withered body
that doesn't know how to leave
or isn't talking. I who don't pray
want to prayer you to the next
world, wondering will I be this
stubborn? Let x come. Let y.
Knowing is overrated. Allow
moths the light that parches them
to paper. Your throat rattles. I kneel
down and welcome it, the what
might take you. Rock in my pocket,
much of you in my textile, extra
mile, rigid right. Ride the wave,
gorge and mark. Then, as if
it were simple, go.

Not Simple

(Before I gingerly pry his lips open, he asks)

> *Is this a one-way street?*

I don't know, it depends what you mean.
(His eyes flit the shadows on the ceiling)

> *I mean, are you allowed to go both ways?*

Yes, but the nurse said to go this way.
(I squirt the morphine under his slugtongue)
(His eyes soar through the ceiling, then to me)

> *Are you wearing a wig?*

(Fingers worry the blanket, pick at his face)
Remember how Mom used to finger-pleate her pants?

> *Are you real?*

(I offer his hands my hair)

> *Someone help! Get me a chair!*

Maybe later, Dad.
(One arm stretches toward the night window,
lifts his shoulder off the bed)

> *I see a room.*

(Now both arms. Eyes, straining, follow)
What does it look like?
(Thinking the words *many* and *mansions*)

> *Who's that?*

Where?

> *Over there, in the corner, by the—*
> *what's THAT?*

Nothing, it's just me and you here.

> *You can't see it?*

No. What do you see?

You're not protecting me!

You're safe, you're—

The cover is coming off my watch!

Do you want to take it off? Is it hurting?

Get me out of here. I don't know why
you won't take me home!

(Voice ever-sharp; arms dance longing)

Is the garage door locked?

Yes. How are your pillows?

Hahaha, you're a big dog!

I'm a dog?

No, not you.

Your mouth looks dry. How about some water?

Hydrate. They said hy-drate.

Yes—no, suck in, not out. That's it, good job.

Why so twisty and turny?

What are you seeing?

Just don't touch things, Ellen.
You're gonna goof it up more.

What?

The cables. C-a-b-l-e-s.

Okay. Is that what you're reaching for?

Don't be silly.

Can I help you with something?
(One arm, then the other)
What do you see?

Your head is all over the place.

Where's *your* head? What do you see?

Almost. I see almost.

We All

We all eat the sun.
And fear footfalls—though not the right ones.
(Blanket of snow, blanket of feathers.)
Where are our mothers?

We fear footfalls—though not the right ones.
Once we own our own itch-scratch
Whither our withering mothers?
Blame it on the tilt of the earth.

Once we own our own itch-scratch
We look for another.
Blame it on the tilt of the earth,
Geese and their song know where they're going.

We look for another other,
Whether bundling up or stripping down.
Geese and their song know where they're going.
Footfalls bode both love and menace.

Bundling up, stripping down,
The precise color of demure matures.
Where are our mothers?
We're born solo and sentient,

though light-years from demure, mature.
They say trees are as good as money.
But are they sentient
At the moment of felling?

They say trees are as good as mothers.
(Solo of snow, solo of feathers.)
At the moment of felling,
We all eat the sun.

No Ode

to greed. Or even need. Wish neither on
no one. I'm in the dentist's chair, numb
to aching, wanting it over, thinking about

want. I want, I'll say it, a certain kind (not certain)
fame, I want not ease not in work but from worry
(that means money), I want never to be x-ed

or y-ed, I want (more) old beautiful stuff
and my house cleaned and to see at least one
wild creature per day and to stop spilling my wine.

I want I want. Whiter teeth and a waist again.
I want a certain boy from 1967 to think of me
and be stirred. Want want want won't. Definitely

don't want this relentless fine spray up my nose,
crook in my neck. Nothing numeric or generic.
Nothing more from Della than what she is. Not

to be found wanting or need to be right. I want
transportation. Via time, place, taste. To be an ear,
give a hand. Grant me modest wishes. Occasional

lightning. To see, in the four-handed dance
between drill and suction, beauty. To want nothing
more from the stars than to stand under them.

Kids Know

Kids know sleep doesn't exist until it takes them
        and they can be taken. Kids own
the questions, like to be the wind.

The moon last night only seemed to be skating
        the clouds. Sometimes the truth
reverses the magic trick. Where does

a kid's first lie come from? How did mine know
        to throw a blanket over her head
when she had hard things to say?

I say underestimation is an adult thing.
        Scientist asks bonobo:
You ready to play? Bonobo: *Past ready.*

Kids know how hide & seek bores us
        and how we hide, divert. *Songbirds*
eavesdrop to survive, I told her—why

don't I don't remember if she was
        surprised? All we know or think we know
—a cleaver we hold over their sweet-smelling heads.

When my parents matter-of-factly warned
        that a boy and girl left alone in a room
will have sex, I couldn't decide—preposterous

or the best news yet? But I knew if the Russians
        pushed the button, I'd find John Bakey
and do whatever the it of sex was. Maybe

it was like being a pair of whirling pinwheels,
        maybe like having church inside you.
Kids' secret-keeping talents spring from what,

and in proportion to who? Their eyes are
        mirrors, which is why we put them to bed
early. That, and exhaustion. Little badgers.

Roustabouts who are not bored until they learn
        to be. Beginners Minds with benefits: being
is not a choice. Kids know they are animals. Weather.

Word

Nightsmell of sweet-aged wood, and curtains
are a breathing. Wet palm of wave gentle-slaps
thighsand. Not like yesterday's brutal. The ribs
of the room with their generous. Resting places.
I understand where *charity* comes from, but *clarity?*
(No no-see-ums here in the white float of almost
sleep.) Looking for a word, I've stepped into a boat.
I want eager. Pray me. *Astonishment*. I'm courting
this best of abstractions. It says: *Look at the fish.*

Ode to Awe

I was going to say
way outsized
excitement, but out-
side says it better:
pond of stars framed
by a circle of high
boughs, the sound
of ice calving, even
the rumbling volcano
that stayed shrouded
our whole two days.
A Russian fox, trusting
humans to remove
a jar from her head.
Tree-shapes pleading
or thrusting, it doesn't
take a Sequoia
to stop me. I disagree
with the dictionary—
it's not fear, but a brief
release from it. In-
human. Bison. Big
water. Light arriving.
If I ever see God,
it'll be out of doors.
I turn the mat around
to say *Welcome*
as I leave.

Notes

"The Night Doesn't Summarize the Day" takes its title from the first line of Dean Young's "Elemental" (*Fall Higher*).

"Ode to Pleasure"—The "wise man" quoted in the last stanza is Alfred Rucker.

"If Dancing" closes with a reference to Mark Seliger's photographs of Merce Cunningham's hands taken in 2009, the year of his death.

"Too-Big November" is for Emma Rose Coleman (1992-2011) and began with Walker Evans's *Kitchen Wall, Alabama Homestead* (gelatin silver print, 1936).

"Field Guide to Abstractions" draws liberally from a talk given by writer and naturalist Tony Eprile at The Hermitage Artist Retreat.

"Lifeboats"— Thank you, NPR.

"True & False" is a "Golden Shovel Poem," a form invented by Terrance Hayes, in which the last words of each line consist, in order, of a line or lines of a poem by Gwendolyn Brooks, in this case "Truth."

"Eyes bat open to dog-yips" takes place in Truchas, New Mexico on October 25, 2012, as Hurricane Sandy is bearing down on the East coast.

"Hearing Aids" is for Charles Cutler, whose words close the poem.

"All I Can Think of Is the Assault Weapon in Some Someone's Hands" began as a response to the line "What's done cannot be undone" from *Macbeth* and to the 2014 Connecticut law that re-categorized the failure to register an assault weapon from a felony to a misdemeanor.

"It Began with the Ping-Pong Balls" features, among other late-night finds, *Top Goon: Diaries of a Little Dictator*, a series of YouTube finger-puppet vignettes created by anonymous Syrian artists to mock Bashar al-Assad.

"Soul Sister Sonnet: Poet to Poet" is for Barbara Ras.

"Women for the World" was commissioned by Smith College for its Women for the World Campaign, for a fine letterpress broadside designed and illustrated by Barry Moser. I'm indebted to poet friends for critiques that helped me meet a tight deadline: Eleanor Wilner, Barbara Ras, Deborah Gorlin, Joan Houlihan, Diana Gordon, Lynne Francis, and Alicia Ostriker. It is dedicated to the women who appear in the poem:

> The girl whose mother has AIDS, and the only fictional character in the poem, is Chanda, the protagonist of the South African film *Life, Above All*, directed by Oliver Schmitz (in Sotho, with English subtitles), and adapted from the YA novel *Chanda's Secrets*, by Canadian author Allan Stratton.

Kazuko Sasaki co-founded the group of Japanese seniors who volunteered to clean up the Fukushima nuclear reactor after the 2011 earthquake and tsunami. She did so because the cells of older people divide more slowly than would those of the younger engineers slated for the work, and because "My generation …promoted the nuclear plants. If we don't take responsibility, who will?"

Dame Daphne Sheldrick created the David Sheldrick Wildlife Trust (named for her late husband) at the northern rim of Kenya's Nairobi National Park, where she has been caring for elephants for over three decades. The film *Born to be Wild* was made about her work (and that of Primatologist Birute Galdikas).

Lise Meitner was the first to discover nuclear fission—with Otto Hahn (who received the 1944 Nobel Prize for the discovery).

Alabaman inventor Mary Anderson started out as a real estate developer, rancher, and viticulturist. In 1903 she was granted her first patent for an automatic car window-cleaning device called the windshield wiper.

Bette Nesmith Graham invented white out while she was executive secretary to the Chairman of the Texas Bank and Trust; she went on to found the Liquid Paper Company.

Dame Cicely Saunders (1918–2005) introduced the idea of "total pain," which included physical, emotional, social, and spiritual distress, and founded St. Christopher's in London—the first modern hospice. Nurse, social worker, and physician, she started a worldwide movement to provide compassionate care for the dying and her work led to the development of a new medical specialty, palliative care.

Polish-American chemist Stephanie Kwolek invented poly-paraphenylene terephtalamide—better known as Kevlar.

Aerospace engineer and aerodynamicist Donna Shirley was the first woman to head up a project for NASA, spearheading the development of Sojourner, the Mars Pathfinder's rover, first to explore the surface of Mars (July 4, 1997).

Marie Tucek patented the first brassiere in 1893; in 1913, Socialite Mary Phelps Jacob patented the first bra to be widely used; Russian immigrant Ida Rosenthal founded Maidenform in 1922 and was responsible for inventing cup sizes.

While the spilling of hot tea in the lap of the man chosen to be her husband was reportedly "accidental," Nawal El Saadawi, born in a small village in Egypt, went on to become a feminist writer, activist, physician and psychiatrist. Author of many books about women in Islam, particularly on the practice of female genital cutting, she is founder and president of the Arab Women's Solidarity Association and co-founder of the Arab Association for Human Rights.

In 2009 Yevgeniya Chirikova, housewife and independent mayoral candidate in the Moscow suburb of Khimki, was removed from the ballot for technicalities deemed "ludicrous and contrived." Chirikova was the leader of a group attempting to stop construction of a superhighway through a pristine stretch of the Khimki Forest. In 2010 President Medvedev shocked the country by ordering an immediate halt to the highway's construction.

"Not a Thing" owes its impulse to a line from the essay "Write Till You Drop," by Annie Dillard: "You were made and set here to give voice to this, your own astonishment."

"Some music" is for Dave Eggar, cellist, pianist and composer. On the first day of a residency at the MacDowell Colony, he spontaneously offered to play cello for the audio recording being made of my fourth poetry collection, *Dogged Hearts* (Tupelo Press, 2010).

"Kids Know" is for Della. The bonobo in question is named Kanzi (Swahili for "buried treasure") and lives at the Great Ape Trust in Des Moines, Iowa, where Dr. Sue Savage-Rumbaugh has taught him to "speak" by pointing at symbols on a large computer screen.

Recent Titles from Alice James Books

ALICE JAMES BOOKS has been publishing poetry since 1973. The press was founded in Boston, Massachusetts as a cooperative wherein authors performed the day-to-day undertakings of the press. This collaborative element remains viable even today, as authors who publish with the press are also invited to become members of the editorial board and participate in editorial decisions at the press. The editorial board selects manuscripts for publication via the press's annual, national competition, the Alice James Award. AJB remains committed to its founders' original mission to support women poets, while expanding upon the scope to include poets of all genders, backgrounds, and stages of their careers. In keeping with our efforts to foster equity and inclusivity in publishing and the literary arts, AJB seeks out poets whose writing possesses the range, depth, and ability to cultivate empathy in our world and to dynamically push against silence. The press was named for Alice James, sister to William and Henry, whose extraordinary gift for writing went unrecognized during her lifetime.

Designed by Dede Cummings

DCDESIGN

Printed by McNaughton & Gunn